How to Create a Blog

A Beginner's Essential Guide for Creating a Blog from Scratch

by Aaron Bantry

Table of Contents

Introduction

The internet has proven that you don't have to be rich or powerful to have your voice heard by the world. And thanks to how simple computer software has become in recent years, you don't have to be a programming whiz kid or a coding savant to create your own blog.

However, while creating a blog is almost as easy as a walk in the park, many misconceptions, poor planning, and novice trip-ups are usually responsible for a blog never seeing the light of day or making it past the first step of the creation process.

And, *that's* where this book comes in. I hereby present to you a comprehensive compilation of expertise garnered through a decade of blogging in the format of an easy-to-follow 5-step process to create a blog from scratch. This is exactly the type of book that I wish had been available to me when I first started on this journey.

Whatever the purpose of your wanting to create a blog: whether it's to have your voice heard, your content aired and enjoyed, your stories read, your poems recited, or just to have your personal life experience out there to help others, years from now I guarantee that you're going to be very grateful you started today.

So, are you ready to learn exactly how to start your own blog? Are you ready to create your own written journey, chronicled for others to see on the hallowed pages of the World Wide Web? Then let's get going!

Chapter 1: Why Blog?

Now there are several reasons why people start their own blog. But, I believe that the *most* important factor why a blog is vital for everyone in this day and age is that it lets you gain control over your own *public* voice in the most heavily inhabited information network in the world—the internet.

With this increasingly smaller world, through the magic of technology, and the disconnect of public forums with physical spacing and locations, an undeniably large amount of intelligence and opinion sharing takes place over the radio waves of the internet. And with this phenomenon also comes the effect of secluding anyone who hasn't got complete control over their own platform and voice from the rest of the civilized world. So, although social media networks allow for short information-sharing opportunities, blogs allow you to create an entire visual and aural experience for your audience.

In those terms, having a blog is like having a home where you can invite people over for a chat. You can choose the different elements, from the wallpaper to the drapes and the music to the food you serve, which allow you to infuse the surroundings in which your opinion is shared with your own distinct personality and flavor. While some people may argue that many social media networks allow the same sharing of information through features such as posted "notes", the overall effect in those cases is more akin to inviting people to a hotel's banquet hall for a talk—your words and opinions may be in your own hands, but they could get heavily censored depending on the establishment under which you pitch your umbrella, and the surroundings or the sensations they impart aren't in your hands in the least bit. And it's the overall experience which counts most for visitors, and not just the textual food for thought.

Another reason why a blog is crucial is that simply concentrating on 9 to 5 jobs today just isn't good enough to build a dream lifestyle for many in the 21st century. Financial sense dictates that, apart from active incomes, we should also create several sources of passive income that would bolster personal revenues and provide for a fallback as buffers for the invariable ups and downs of life. And even if you manage to run just a decently regular blog, let alone an orgasmically distinguished one, *that* is precisely what you'll create.

Moreover, the age of Knights is long gone, and we now live in the age of Kings—where intellect, sophistication, charisma, leadership, eloquence, and charm are the winning qualities, not survival instincts or brawn. Therefore, a third reason why blogs become part and parcel of any successful 21st century citizen's repertoire is the indubitable effect they have on communication and linguistic skills. Start-up blogs are essentially like the lemonade and hot-dog stands of the internet world—personalized shadows of the "dot com" bubble age which came at a time where the world wasn't yet prepared for them.

So, if your experience over time allows you to better understand your base clientele, and the sort of crowd which you wish to attract to your blogs, the different avenues which open up for you—among entertainment, retail sales, article aggregation and content distribution, etc.—are innumerable. In this manner, not only do they allow you to perform hands-on market research as you tweak and twist your offerings over the years, but they also allow you to work on those all-important communication skills through the variety of content which you put up as you go along. And as we already know—awesome communication skills are 80% of the battle for success in this global arena.

Additionally, blogging is one of the most essential ways to attract and retain customers today—for both small and large businesses. Gone are the times when the product was the only thing that mattered—we now live in an era where people want to invest in firms by purchasing their services, and not just perform a give-and-take transaction. With that in mind, blogs allow you to showcase your expertise through your opinions, and form a connection with your audience or prospective clientele by initiating a discussion.

The *entire* world of business depends on a single principle—someone has a problem, and they use your services and products to get rid of that problem. Blogs allow you to demonstrate your cognitive reasoning, rationale, and experience in whichever area of life that forms the basis of your content. Have a relationship blog? Wrote a great article on cheating partners through your own reasoning and experience? Gave great advice to a particularly depressed visitor? Awesome. Guess what? That visitor just tweeted to fifty of her buddies about that amazing new relationship blog she discovered, and you may soon have twenty-five new regulars popping in to read your stuff every day. Out of these twenty-five, ten might probably buy your new ebook, and another four might spring for that quirky new limited offer tee-shirt you just attached to your brand.

It hardly even matters the kind of business you may run, or even if your blog is strictly personal, it is an outlet which is validated in its value by the world at large, it allows you to make more money if you choose to do so, grant you the opportunity to build your own brand with the flavor of your own personality, and create a sweet audience which interacts with you and challenges your notions of life as you do the same to them. It's a pretty sweet deal for something which takes very little time to create, and just a little bit of dedication to maintain.

Most importantly, in the end, decently successful bloggers are maestros of marketing techniques, people who can identify a market, create a product, inject that product comfortably into a niche, and are editors, writers, SEO experts, and effective salespeople all rolled into one—and who wouldn't want *that* on the personal skills section of their resume? Especially since interface platforms like WordPress render programming skills or other coding knowledge pretty moot to run a great-looking website.

Chapter 2: Choosing Your Content and Writing Style

The reason why I've decided to tackle this particular topic before moving on to the choice of platforms is that knowing your content and writing style will probably impact your platform choice quite strongly.

The very first thing which you need to decide is the niche or category in which you wish to contribute content. Basically, is this going to be a gaming blog, or about relationships, food, business, finance, technology, science, or some other topic? For starters, I wouldn't recommend throwing in too many niche topics into the mix. This is mainly to get a good content base and search engine rank. The best blog content in the world is just as worthless as horrifically badly-written ones if neither of them manage to draw in visitors—and that's just the harsh truth.

If you like juggling many balls at once, I would suggest picking your single most favorite niche out of the handful which excite you—because you're going to *really* need that to keep up with the content demands—and then add more categories to your blog site after a year or two, once you build up a decent visitor base and daily unique hits. Just to clarify, unique hits mean incoming traffic from different IP addresses—so returning visitors don't count towards this number.

Once you've identified your base niche category, you need to specify it further—is this going to be an opinion blog, or will it deal with news, formulate new ways or avenues of discussion, humor, satire? So, going with the same example of the relationship blog, would you rather just talk about your own experiences? Or your experiences with a sarcastic twist in your writing? Or use it as an outlet to vent? Or create funny but gripping content based on observations about the strange elements of every relationship? Do you want to start an advice column? Or create a forum where other people who suffer hurts through relationships can openly discuss their issues without direction or content-based leads from you? Your blog should have a very specific purpose in mind. There are plenty of "Jack of all trades" websites out there which are already well-established, and your only way of competing with them is to find an angle which makes you the Master of that particular "one".

After you're convinced of your choice of blogging content, the next thing which you need to identify is your prospective blogging schedule. Now, I would like to say that everyone who makes a resolution to deliver "X" blogs per week sticks to it with their first blog. But, sadly, that's not always—or even mostly—the case.

The first blog usually ends up like the first pancake, the chimeric product of erroneous trials which is usually thrown into the bin. However, here's how you'll differ from those people—this guide will already tell you the basic mistakes to avoid. The good part about that is that when people throw away their first blog and make a new one after a while, they've already lost out 90% of their visitors who landed on their content by chance, liked it, and spread the word around to their circles. These visitors are precious because they are often quite removed from the author's own circles—many "visiting" from different countries and continents. However, since they stuck out their neck once for such authors, and attached their stamp of approval when discussing said blog with their friends only to have the blog close down, they would be loathe to do so again.

You, on the other hand, by getting your first blog right, will hold on to all those distinct visitors and reap the benefits of the explosive rise in popularity which they provide. It *is* a global market after all on the internet, and the whole world's your hunting ground.

Anyway, when identifying your schedule, you need to decide the number of hours you can devote to your blog per week and make the best effort to stick to that once you create a routine. This is basically useful in determining whether you just wish to be a casual blogger, an avid one, devote equal times to your blogging and other aspects of your life, or if you wish to create a future through your blog. I'll discuss the implications of these choices on your pick of platform in the next chapter.

On top of all that, you also need to decide the *tone* of your blog. Now, by tone, I mean the style of content which you wish to offer. Would it be graphic? Or push the boundaries of civilized conversation? These are perfectly good tones to have—in fact, many people owe their entire careers to the fact that they refused to play by society's rules, censorship ideals, and taboos. However, that also means that you need to work in a virtual space which offers you more freedom and creative control, rather than one where you could possibly fall under the censorship hammer of another individual or organization. We will also discuss the implications of your style in the next chapter.

Chapter 3: Selecting the Right Platform

Let me start by saying this—I *love* WordPress platforms, and the freedom of having my own self-hosted websites. I won't necessarily defend that point of view, because I believe that favoring one mode over another would violate the spirit of this book, but I will present the pros and cons of the various blogging platforms in this chapter.

So, let's begin by addressing the needs of the very casual, rarely engaged, barely regular bloggers who wish to create their own content either to serve as an outlet for their own voice, opinions, and emotions which run amok in daily life, or to test the blogging waters by dipping their toes in the audience pool and testing the feedback response. There's nothing wrong with fulfilling such needs through a beginner's casual blogging experience—the World Wide Web is filled to capacity with millions of blogs, and roughly 60% of all of them fall within this category.

Such people often don't have a lot of time to spare, and just wish for a simple space on the internet to showcase their works or vent their emotions. Many fine poets, writers, literary comedians, etc., started their journeys in a similar fashion—by building up confidence in themselves through casual blogging before they were ready to delve into it with regularity.

The first, and somewhat unorthodox, option here is to use Facebook. Yes, the gargantuan social media modern-day equivalent of the old Yellow pages directory. The "Notes" option within Facebook allows you to create and post content within your own circles, with all the marketing tools which would allow your network to "Like" and "Share" your work with others, if they choose to do so. This allows people, who don't have the desire or drive to spend an hour creating a blog, to first check and hone their skills if they wish to do so in a familiar environment. Also, Facebook offers several RSS apps and services which you can go through, subscribe to, or pay for, to get your posts published on wider networks and draw in bigger audiences.

The second option is using free blogging platforms such as Blogger.com, WordPress.org, Tumblr, etc. These platforms allow you to create a simple blog for yourself within their own directory and network, in which you get simple thematic options for visuals that allow you to focus on your content.

The problem with these options is that they are patently useless if you wish for your blog to have a long-term future of its own, and if you want to use it to create and enhance your own brand. These platforms give you little control over your own domain name, with URLs often being clunky and rather ugly. If that seems like a small problem, tell me the last time you saw a website called "susanteachesyoutocookwell.blogger.com" and went "Wow, what a great name. I'll remember that forever"?

When faced with names such as Sorted or TheDailyMeal, the other name rather pales by comparison—pretty much guaranteeing the fact that three days later you'd be Googling for other culinary blogs since you couldn't remember the name of "Susan's Whatever" if your life depended on it. Names are the first aspect of a brand, and they stick with your blogging creation for life. Although you *could* technically move to other blogs later on, and transfer your audience there, it would almost certainly lose you quite a significant portion of your daily visitors—not to mention your old search engine rank. So, while it *can* be done, I would strongly avoid planning in this manner if you *do* aim to have a long-term blog. It's far more efficient to lay the proper groundwork into your own website from the get-go.

Another problem with blogging platforms is that their offerings in terms of themes, added services, and other features which would allow you to add your own glorious touches are horrendously limited. You'll more likely than not end up with rather amateurish looking blogs which **scream** "I don't know what I'm doing, so don't waste your time on me." In such cases, it's *almost* better to just use social media platforms as a *sort-of* blog 'til you're ready to invest more effort into it.

The last problem with these platforms is *ownership*. While you own your content, you **do not** actually own your blog—that vital power still resting firmly in the hands of the platform itself. This means that if you intend to push the envelope and tackle serious problems in manners which may either raise controversy, or indulge in content which may not strictly-speaking be legal or conform to the ethical practices of the platform, you'll wake up one day to find all of your work deleted, and your blog having vanished from the face of the web in a silent *poof*. Even if you *weren't* planning on dealing in controversy within your content, that aspect of censorship would still raise the hackles of many artistic or literary folk on principle alone.

The next set of options deal with people who wish to try out blogging quite seriously, but either don't have the finances to invest in a paid hosting service or don't wish to do so just yet. For such people, who still wish to own their own domain name and website, one valid option is to use free hosting sites such as x10hosting.com, etc. What these sites allow you to do is to register with them and receive a free domain name which would be hosted by them on the internet for no charge whatsoever, for a year. They also offer extra services such as easy one-click installation of WordPress packages to serve as the basic interface of your website, and offer different options such as market retailer, forums, blogs, and other templates—depending on your chosen purpose.

However, while it's sinfully easy to use and launch a website through such services, the downsides crop up from the second year onwards. Once the free year is up, you will probably be faced with a continuation fee which is significantly higher than the average marker payment per year for the hosting service. At this point, it usually becomes quite clear that the economically sensible thing to do is to start a new website using other paid services if you don't wish to pay larger sums of money to continue with your old domain name—and so again, you stand to lose all the effort you put into it for the past year and getting it up through the search engine ranks.

Moreover, while they offer a wide range of domain names, and don't insist on uglifying the URLs by adding their own name in the middle, the choice of good names with respectable domain suffixes are in severely short supply which make it harder for you to pick a good name with the ".com" suffix in tow. Instead, chances are that you'll have to end up with second-rate suffixes like .org, .tk, .nz, and so on and so forth—which is enough to turn off many prospective visitors and clients for the perceived lack of professionalism. Understand this: ".**com**"s rule the domain name world for a good reason. Without any significant evidence or rationale behind this, dot coms carry extra weight of perceived quality control, even though no such controls exist in reality, simply because they stand for "United States Commercial Website". So, if you're a business wishing to launch your own blog, or a blogger hoping to create your own brand, a dot com is a must-have for you.

And this brings us to the last set of options—paid hosting services such as GoDaddy, SquareSpace, etc. Now, the first illusion that I must dispel is that good hosting sites charge you a kidney and a leg for their product. In fact, many great services barely charge over $2-$3/month. And this cost falls significantly if you directly opt for 12 month packages or more right from the get-go. In addition, they provide you with greater range of domain names, and even offer to buy ones which you may like but may not be available within their registry by contacting the current owners with price bids. Once you've chosen the domain name, they complete registration processes with registrars for you, and even provide you with customer service options, webinars and other features to increase the core brand value of your website, etc.

Moreover, they offer the same WordPress interfaces with gigantic libraries of themes to choose from—and this is in addition to the monstrously huge databases of free and paid WordPress theme makers, plug-ins, and other apps which are openly accessible for download through the internet. Lastly, they also provide greater security, and have no form of censorship exerted upon the people choosing to opt for their services, which severely reduces chances of frivolous deletion or censorship—unless you break the laws of the country in which they reside, and a formal court order is issued against your name.

All in all, though there are plenty of blogging options available—none of which take longer than an hour at the most to set up and launch—the best options for people with long-term plans or brand aspirations are the paid ones. After all, even when you need to renew your hosting plans—though the prices may go up since the first year—they will be far more stringently controlled, and much cheaper than the "free hosts". In the end, the only factor which affects your choice of platform is your short- and long-term plans regarding your future with your blog. Also, if you plan ahead and aim to sell your branded blog in the future, these small payments will be worth hundred-fold in the long run. If you don't believe me, just Google the richest bloggers in the world.

Chapter 4: Creating Your Blog

Compared to the rest of the principal decisions which you need to make in this entire process, actually *creating* your blog is by far the simplest thing you will have to do. But first, the most important hurdle that you need to cross is choosing the name for your blog. Regardless of your choice of platform, except social media sites such as Facebook of course, your name will determine brand recognition, and ultimately its value. As I proved through the example before, there is much more to a name than just a random collection of letters.

A good name fulfills three basic needs—it embodies the core concept of your blog and displays its purpose without confusion or ambiguity; it is memorable and catchy, even if it is burdened by longer URLs through blogging platforms; it serves as a respectable basis for a brand name, since you will have to stick with it for a while. So, in the example we had used earlier, even "susanskitchen.blogger.com", "susanspantry.blogger.com", "foodart.blogger.com" or any of several variations would have served better as a name than the original. Small touches can make a big difference in a name, and less is always more. If you can sum up the entire philosophy of your blog in a single word, that's the best path you can take for your blog name. This is primarily why I love the name

"Sorted" for the website run by a couple of British blokes who tackle elegant cuisine for everyday use—because they "sort" or successfully handle those dishes and show their audience how to incorporate seemingly difficult food easily into everyday life, while respecting the restricted time available when cooking such dishes for everyday use. That's a mouthful of a philosophy, and it fits pretty well into a single word. Fulfill that checklist, come up with a great name, and it will *literally* halve your workload in marketing your blog. Depending on the name and suffix you pick, check again and yet again for the availability of that name on the platform which you've finally picked. If your selected name isn't available, you can either pick a different variation of the name, pick a different suffix for the domain (something other than .com; not recommended for long term planning), or check with different platform services.

Once that step is done, all you need is to fill in your information into the website's application form, choose whatever packages appeal to you if you wish to pay (check for discount coupons and offer codes on the internet; often available through other famous users of the same service), and get out through the other end to land on your *very own website*. If and when you receive the option to choose an interface, *always go for WordPress*. This is simply because, in terms of ease of use and availability of free tools and plug-ins, absolutely nothing beats WordPress.

After choosing the interface, and landing on your website's landing page, you can log into its back-end processes to finally put your blog together. The first thing which you'll need to do is to pick a theme for your site. Now, the theme is basically an arrangement of backgrounds, foregrounds, plug-in layouts etc. This will determine how your pictures look (if you post any), what background choices you have available, the extent to which you can customize titles and headers, and a lot more.

While you may find many to your liking in the basic library accessible through WordPress itself, you can also check online for an exhausting amount of free choices available for download through the websites of WordPress theme developers. Spend as much time on this particular step as you feel you need, because the *look* of a blog makes all the difference between "professional, inviting, and attractive" and "cheap, two-bit, ugly jobs" even if you haven't actually paid a cent for the site. Pick themes that suit your categories, writing styles, and personality *altogether*. This particular choice would be as important as the scent of your dish wafting over to you as the waiter approaches with his tray—it *literally* whet's a visitor's appetite for your content, and forms the very first impression in their overall experience.

Once you've decided on the titles, headers, themes, etc.—you are now ready to write, post, and publish content. However, before you get too pleased with yourself and forget some important steps—you need to add a few plug-ins before your job here is done for now. The very first thing which you need to add is a good security plug-in, and an efficient SEO plug-in. There are hundreds of free ones available within the WordPress libraries, including some of the very best the world has to offer. You honestly won't need to pay for great plug-ins when their work can be effectively fulfilled by really awesome free ones.

You can also Google the best ones in each category for complete lists, reviews, comments, customer feedbacks, and easy instructions for installation. Which brings us to another point—every installation within WordPress can be easily completed with a single click. All you need to do is to use search engines for the ones you wish to integrate into your blog, and then search for them from within the WordPress search present in your website's settings. There are several easy guides and "How-To"s available that teach you how to use such plug-ins in comprehensive detail as well, often made by the creators of the plug-ins themselves.

The other essential plug-in which you need to add is one which integrates your blog with social media websites. These usually come in two forms—the ones which allow sharing, and the ones which allow subscription. The first category of plug-ins will allow your visitors to like, tweet and share your content on these sites through their own profiles, while the second set will integrate your own social media information to allow interested visitors to follow you on Facebook, Twitter, etc.

If you wish to interact with your visitors, you also need to add a "Comments" plug-in. While my personal recommendation in this regard is to use Disqus, there are many others which are lighter that may serve your immediate needs as well. However, the filter options and approval choices available through higher-quality plug-ins like Disqus will be invaluable to you within a short period, once you start facing the auto-bot comment spam trash which invariably crawls from site to site on the internet.

The last touch which you need to complete before you close up for the day is to link your site to Google Analytics, and to submit your site's link to Google for search engine ranking. The first of these is a free feature which requires registration and allows you to track your incoming traffic in detail from across the globe. Simply follow the detailed instructions on the Google Analytics page to integrate it with your own website's settings dashboard, and wait for a day or two for it to compile enough information for analysis. Once this is up and running, it will give you a clear view of your number of daily hits, unique visitors, country and city of origin, etc.

The second among these would require you to add appropriate plug-ins to create a site map which would then be submitted to search engines. However, several SEO plug-ins will have in-built features which would allow you to do that from within them without needing more plug-ins that would conk your system and weigh down the speed of your website loading times.

With this, your website is completely up and functional, and ready for you to launch your content.

Chapter 5: How to Market and Gain an Audience

If great content alone could have spelled success for a blog, this would have been a very different world indeed. And so—regardless of whether you're a casual blogger, or one determined to make a name for yourself through this course of action—you need to market the living daylights out of your content. This means that you need to remember and be acutely aware of the time in a day when most of your target audience would be likely to be sitting on their social media, and use those time periods to initially launch your posts and share them through Facebook, Twitter, etc. This would increase the chances of visibility for your content share within those crowded and constantly-updating home page feeds.

This will become less important as you pick up a global audience and build a decent daily visitor count. However, if you've created a schedule for yourself—9 PM on Tuesdays, and the same time on Thursdays, for example—you need to stick to it, come hell or high water. Your own audience will often try to make time for you in their own schedules if they enjoy your blogs. But to do so, they need to be able to rely on a regular time and date when to expect new updates from you. Hell hath no fury, like readers spending their office-break expecting the much-awaited new post from you which doesn't appear by its scheduled time.

The second part of this is that when you share your new posts on social media, you're essentially selling your content's appeal to people who haven't tried it yet. This step isn't really aimed at your regular readers, since all they need is an update from you. So, you need to develop that thick skin needed to shamelessly market your product through every "share" if you wish to see any decent growth. While this may be more difficult at first, practice and experience will sharpen these skills to a honed edge with time.

Conclusion

There are several nuances concerned with the art of blogging which are rather hard to teach or explain, and can only truly be mastered through experience. However, for a first blog, this book should more than set you up with all the information you need to build an amazing launch pad for your blogging career.

In keeping with the spirit of keeping you ahead of the normal learning curve, here's another pointer you need to keep in mind. The more often you choose to post new content, the faster will be your growth. Sounds sort of Yoda-ish, but it's simple search engine magic. More content means more keywords, higher traffic, which leads to higher search engine ranks, which drives even *more* traffic to your website. Moreover, if your content is good and you're quite prolific with your output rate, people would be more inclined to recommend you to others while checking in on your website everyday as well.

In order to do this, and keep up with output demands while avoiding unnecessary pressure from deadlines, successful bloggers always have two to three posts ready to go at any point of time, which they then upload and schedule for auto-publishing at future dates. In this manner, you could be outside and enjoying a party while your website is launching your new post, sharing it on your social media network, and adding pre-written messages to go along with each "share". Not only would this improve your blogging discipline and allow you to enjoy your life outside, but it would mean that blogging never cuts into your other needs and responsibilities.

As a final note, I wish to share that becoming a successful blogger is 30% content, 20% consistency, 10% constant improvement, 10% tech-savvy and eye for aesthetics, and 30% sheer grit and determination. However, roughly 8 out of every 10 bloggers abandon their regular schedule, and thus effectively stop the phenomenal growth of their audience through the initial momentum within the first month and a half of starting their blog. It becomes exponentially more difficult to pick up that momentum again in the future through the same website. So, get through those first months, make blogging a regular part of your life and you'll already be in the top 20% of blogs in the world—regardless of content. It really is that simple.

Finally, I'd like to thank you for purchasing this book! If you enjoyed it or found it helpful, I'd greatly appreciate it if you'd take a moment to leave a review on Amazon. Thank you!

Made in the USA
Middletown, DE
29 May 2017